If you cannot understand these words, I write in this specific order then I will let you see. this specific order has not been common in your eyes to be understood. It however is not the case that I am wrong or that you just cannot understand. The only problem is these words will only brighten the minds of those who seek uncommon knowledge. By listening to the words of uncommon knowledge you will stumble upon uncommon light.

Chapter 1

If your words you have written for one to see other than yourself have been denied by the evil in the mind, of all who walk upon Earth. we all will see that there is no resemblance between the heart in our chest along with our brain on top of all irrelevant body parts. These irrelevant items of the body will only be as I say if my words will inform the unnoticed mind.

When I refer to the word of evil or devil in the mind, I am speaking of not conforming to accepted standards of morality. Which in this case, if half of the population do the complete opposite as I do. they will all believe in what they will proceed to do themselves with others and as well will see me as a fool.

with intent to look powerful with themselves to bring them higher Above All Mankind. when the two opposites come together to eat dinner with each other, it will go unnoticed by both sides of Good and Evil. That both sides will indeed eat the fruit from Earth to continue doing what they each look down upon.

This shows me both are blind if they will continue to look down on the one they are eating with. For instance, an herbivore will only eat plants while carnivores will only eat meat an omnivore will eat both meat on top of plants. All the factors related to human kind as we're speaking of not conforming to accepted standards of morality. All three enjoy what they eat and are also seen as evil in the mind of someone who is also seen as evil. Each looking down on all yet are sitting, speaking also eating in their presence.

Now to give the one who looks down on you a piece of meat which they enjoy, although you only eat plants. This act is very pleasing to whomever sees with their eyes you doing so. Yee to the one who is to laugh at their neighbor or to speak of destruction concerning the opposite of their own life. you will surely turn into dust; this is Unholy and the love given to you for the last kind act will be retrieved.

This example I have given is to show you that the man who walks is not to be laughed at. For He Who Walks is doing so for the intent to enjoy this gift he was given. He Who Walks has not looked down on you while going past him, rain will cool his blood. his heart will be even with the steps of pure faith.

You should not speak destruction on others for the Reason Thy have not tried to destroy you. so, he should either accept how a neighbor life or thy shall turn to dust. A very clear reason that speaking hatred on a neighbor is irrelevant to bring forth

Considering that good combined with evil go perfectly together in the case. of doing a task known as impossible, If good and evil love their life. and choose to keep it they will have to take refuge in the opposite side they do not live.

Now for A source of writing many have read in the holy bible. it says (those shall be put to death for murder while the phrase is put forth. A man who injures his countryman — as he has done, so it shall be done to him [namely,] fracture under/for fracture, eye under/for eye, tooth under/for tooth. Just as another person has received injury from him, so it will be given to him." (Lev. 24:19–21).
This shows me these three are examples of injuring a neighbor for instance, if you cut off my finger this will be done to you. I've seen a sentence in this same book Proverbs 12:18. (there is one whose rash words are like sword thrusts yet the tongue of the wise brings healing). by putting these two together I see a sword thrust may actually injure me, just like a word would injure me .

With my knowledge a word has many different scenarios, for a person may say a nice word with the intent to destroy you. a person may use a nice word to be nice to you in a caring Manor. a person may use a hateful word to build you up in a caring way to show you true love. exactly the same as a person using a nice word as to be caring.

A person who can speak a hateful word with the intent for power over you or destroy you solely. to own you will blind themselves if you so choose to let them be Blind. By loving them and accepting all of his hateful or good remarks thy will not only think rightfully. yet they will see their own Fate by getting hurt by any word known to man.

This will not only show you which path you should rather take; it will show how to make both Become One of DeVine. Each person alive will fight for something they would enjoy doing rather it be saving a life or killing one off. Preferably to plant a garden or burning one to ashes. Neither human would want the gift of destroying overpowering, procreating and saving to disappear from their life. nor lose the gift of Consciousness if they knew they could stop it from ending.

rather

you would like to know whether or not having some type of power is why each human would not wish to lose their gift. the power of knowing they destroyed a visible creation or in helping in some way. This was created from the force which created them as well. If you were to cut the grass it will be work to destroy yet it will give life to your eyes for some.

Most likely keep poisonous bugs or Critters from harming your family. This I say to you is an example of Good and Evil in which many are blind of all scenarios of each task you choose on taking fourth. Conforming to accepted standards of morality is what all humans follow or go against without thinking about.

now if someone does, says or follows something that none have seen he will most likely be hated by all who notices him. for no one likes to see something or someone. They haven't had the knowledge or had themselves unless they are pure of mind. many having different gods. Some follow the devil also few will only follow government standards.

Doing it all as they say following their spouse will perceive him as a type of God, I proceed to just keep to myself. by keeping to myself I will see that to have everything known to man is a false term used by the devil in the mind. you will need to understand by grabbing a handful of the softest soil you are now holding the mother of What is that you want or wish to keep. any materialistic item you wish to think of do not be evil by needing. for what is given, is what is in between your fingers.

As I awake this morning, I was speechless as I could function with my eyes, to see objects. very strange indeed I had no recognition of all materialistic items surrounded by me. I had no idea who my own family Was, whoever I did know, where and how it all came together.

I Was Not Afraid until I saw a surprising Force coming at me. This force was slow in time to see myself and to figure out why it would run at me. I will respect the entire situation that had just come into my knowledge. by this certain product of my life being seen by a whole (two four one two B).

It will not only become many different scenarios for me to attend yet by me observing this fateful moment. I will be able to identify exactly how every situation will go by knowing the opposite of thy fate. I will utterly be able to see all outcomes of any situation.

If the plan was to be attempted by only one soul it should not be taken lightly. with this plan, if used for power it will end your life before seen in your own eyesight. it will still be completed however will have been found by you, also attempted. yet it will not mean anything to you once you have gotten what you deserve. so why would it mean anything to anyone, that you had found this divine plan.
                                                          When given life you will take a breath of air not in the intentions of stealing. nor should you feel regret by doing as you so please for good reason. needing to honor the gift given, so for anyone who is needing

the same breath to stay alive. shall not put power over your life, in the case of you following instructions for the fate of their own.

When hidden from all who have seen you only the ones who look in the cracks will find the treasures that lie inside. the ones who see and take the treasure before the cracks will be led astray. for it was easiest to get, and easier to see they will get the easiest path they will turn into dust by their own hand.

you will want a soft, clean hand to hold after doing wrong in front of all who walk. you will indeed hold the hand knowing good and well your hand is rough and dirty With the False truth. you will Shadow the evilness you have brought To Us by asking for a hand to hold.

this is generally non forgivable in the sight of my eyes If this is brought to my door. forgiveness will not be just giving. Yet an explanation also proves there will be no need to do the same in the future.

Let's say for some reason I have planted my own garden barring the ripest boldest fruit on Earth. you come to me, asking for a second chance on being my friend or partner. having in mind that you will get the fruit that will cease your hunger. Indeed, it will cure your hunger, yet this fruit is for the Unworthy, for this fruit will ultimately end your life. if not proven you will grow the fruit yourself with the seeds given in the past. those who will look down upon me and choose not to walk with me if I shall stay.

I will appreciate walking with them, they will not walk with me with the presence of hateful words or bad intentions tied to their back. unholiness is not wanted by ABE, a human will always choose being powerful over others. unless given or shown any opportunity that no one has seen or accomplished.

By accepting this, one will bow to all who live with one knee only one knee. For me getting on two knees is not for the sight of humans. If you are born (someone / a force) has given life to you as for also given their life for yours.

If you will understand the entire meaning to this for instance, Jesus has accepted to die for you for the reason of true love. Inevitably for even getting the chance to know 1 other than him is alive. for you killing him under his eyes it is true love that was shown to him as well. for something that is created to have the need to do something so terrible. it showed him they all truly needed help, that he could give the ultimate help they all needed right in that second this is true love

I had the choice of being condemned to where I could not leave a certain area. my choices were to take the path which would be rough on my brain or to take the path which would be tough on my feet. for me to explain this further can only happen if my brain is calm not my feet.

If I am put in a position to lose a dear loved one by knowing What could happen, if I was to give them what they want, not what I want I already know I will lose them. By doing as they please my mind (brain) will be on a tough Journey as this will not be a calming path to take. me doing this will be treacherous for me in many ways.

my words would have been written with my eyes closed, my pin would have been filled with the blood from the unfaithful. if giving a friend what they want and not as I condone. I can write with both of my feet cut off with myself knowing the consequences of my actions. With myself, forming the actions from past experiences are better for my mind. Also, it will be only what it is I want to be a part of.

I do know right from wrong, what I did by Smashing store Windows may. be wrong for whoever may get the knowledge of me doing so. me choosing to show you a piece of glass Does not mean more to me than the person who will get to see or hear my words. as having them pass through a gate in your brain Is the reason why I choose to have a clear mind.

each letter I write in life is one by pure Faith yet me committing an act of evil in your eyes. is not conforming to accepted terms of morality, are you accepting the death of yourself or anyone you have spoken with? I would call this conforming to accepted terms of morality you accept this, why is that?

ask yourself why you accept dying or watching someone you care for pass away. you say you care for them yet no one has copied my words. It is irrelevant to me knowing how to stop death if no one was to know it existed. for the only way I can tell you that death can be stopped is to know accepted terms of morality only exist because of death.

If all on Earth was to be dead, not one living thing, there would be no good nor bad item on the planet. If we were alive on the planet with the presence of death there will be good and bad. Bad will not like good, Good will not like bad.

there is only one more thing I have not explained would be to not have the Opposites at all. The good one does can be seen as bad and the bad one does can be seen as good. to not have the Opposites of Good and Evil you will indeed have to understand you are not alive to Parish. you are alive to understand the plan which I write about. you will need to respect all in the past that has been done for you to be here rather it be good or bad.

It has been done and cannot be retrieved, not one but many have died for you yet all have lived as well. as they have lived for you and given your life, your life has been worked for by many from the past. They have lost more than they would wish they cared for more for whom was not you. by watching their loved ones slowly die and watching terrible things you haven't seen. It would only be right to live the life they fought and died for.

If I was to get a job cutting down trees(logging) I am doing so to feed my family. Yet what I came to realize as I started to pass out is that I was cutting my oxygen out. also taking oxygen from the lungs of those I'm trying to feed and using the money to buy an apple. Many would say a tree would grow back "that's what they do".

you will kill one of my kids and then one of your friends comes and kills the last kid I have left. then you say make another kid that's what humans do, what's the point in having a baby if you will kill it. I don't accept one to perish for helping me to live, why should I be called evil. I don't accept one disrespecting the gift thy were given, just as all who own a glass window does not accept me smashing it.

I will smash an object you have worked your life for so you can see the one smashing it. only doing so in order to give you the knowledge of knowing you can save us all from dying. an object is an amazing thing yet you all are killing yourselves for before you live to own it.

I often sit in the shadows of Earth when I decided long ago this plan is what I will do for now on.

Anything that comes under my feet is the path I choose only for the greater good. I will watch the path others may take and this will lead to my new staff dust to dust.

if one shall not listen their body will become dust a tree has come from the earth which is dust. A staff is what I will break off of a tree so one day as I find myself again this will be the day you actually get to help me. holding me up so I can find someone who will listen so I can help everyone.

I am not the founder and creator of any knowledge I have shared; it was given to me. I will pass it on to whoever I cross paths with and the plan will be sturdy. No one on earth is DeVine I only know this in the case of seeing death. if one is three and one, they will live forever yet they are not divine. only for the reason that I am not living forever if one was divine, they would share the gift with all who live.

In the case of trusting a dear neighbor to know they will disrespect their gift a second time. if I was to find the way to live forever, would I be a terrible person by not sharing it with all. this would make one who wanted to live even stronger against evil, if done by themselves.

truthfully there are always consequences for actions even if you believe the actions are going to keep your life the same. the actions I'm speaking of has no remark or concern on standing with the one who says he has found a plan. By thinking nothing will change by my plan you will be dust in time. which is still helping for someone can use that dust to form something that will help me.

you will be swallowed by these consequences I will not be saddened or happy of one's death. for that is the path you have taken you may be powerful in your own mind. yet you are not needed if you cannot follow directions of the universe. for this your life so it is irrelevant for me to risk mine.

your family needed your help you have turned your back on all of humans. you will Deserve the Last Breath You Take This will keep ashes of the fresh bonfire sacred for eternity. I would not like to see this happen to any of you, is why I am doing this plan Yee will I cry at your passing.

I will still stand for you as I've said many times many have loved you for eternity. I have found this love I have seen each human be sad for something as of a loss. then they change this into pure hatred when seeing someone happy. as if thy neighbor hasn't lost something dear to them as well.

this could harm the one they are speaking with as also himself. as we both will need to understand it is bad for them. When their ancestors did not listen to someone or something that tried helping. also do you want to be called the ancestor that did not listen. when the time comes and your loved one passes you will be mad at me that I have no remorse.

they died for your actions of greed and self-power in your mind. all is in your hands you should not be sad about this. you should be happy that you were right, aren't you? this is the product of the power you owned. the one that has died now will give you relief that your secrets will be hidden from those who live.

this is what you wanted now you get what you want money, food also a peaceful life. all now is yours; it is too bad you will be dust when you drop your rock. I Will Not Laugh nor be saddened by your passing it will only be my fault for your death. Other deaths will be the blood of your power.

by blinding a neighbor could be how you believe in a certain objective in life. yet you don't fully understand what it is you are passing up .do not lead others to their Ultimate Death by trying to save them. you are speaking blind words before you see them it's like cutting a tree down to buy an apple. I am sitting surrounded by humans who are blind by what they hear and what they believe.

what it is you see is not the entire truth if I see a crack in a wall. also, I tell everyone there is a crack "the ones" who were slipped this message go look at this crack. all are positive by this situation, yet me in the back watching the crowd reactions is only knowledge for me to consume. By me doing this "staying quiet" I will know how everyone chooses to act.

I can act the way each one has done on many different occasions. I will know every word any has spoken; I will also know each movement brought forth by the people. watching the crowd in many different situations, I'll always be in the back to gain knowledge. it's not being bad I am just learning for the future. now since I've done this many times I will know when you're talking about the crack in the wall.

I will wait until all are gone so I can go to the opposite side of the wall. I will see no crack then I will go look at this supposed crack furthermore I will see it is only paint. If I do not tell them, it is paint, the person who said the blind truth to his or her peers. will most likely see it is paint eventually it will teach themselves to not go by what they first see. Yee to go and spread a confused thought by your first thought.

this will Blind themselves also others in many ways than one. I will never be blind by a human's words while I am alive, I will blind myself. if this is how I choose this is what I accept I will live by the terms of good and evil. I will never tell anyone it is better for them Yee will I let them burn. Me thinking of finishing the plan myself, I will be led to see how having a baby will be an amazing gift.

Also Having a marriage is amazing yet if I see them die in front of me having what you want is not really what I want. for If I have nothing, I will lose nothing, now I will give an example. If I have all the money in the world, I will also own the entire world. for this I will indeed lose every known item also will I lose every love. as well so what is the point in having anything at all.

I would just be keeping it sacred for the ones who disrespected it. nothing on Earth is to my possession if these words are close to being destroyed. I will fight knowing I am trying as hard as possible (only to the extent of my heartbeat).

for I know to be quiet and not start a Ruckus among others. It is important to be cotton in front of a rock. only when it's necessary can it be performed, by heart is the one that decides when it is my time to Parish. as it is connected to force unknown to humans.

If one tells you they know what is connected to their heart by explaining it. they have formed this knowledge from dust of the earth and will surely be that dust. to whomever it is concerning I have no knowledge of the force who created me. from a different perspective of your own I only know what I have seen or been through.

you or someone interrupting me by saying I am wrong or telling me their side. This could lead to my death by blinding me. They have deliberately undermined me and have tried to make it impossible for me to finish the plan.

A neighbor's words that says we can never live and nothing can ever change are indeed irrelevant. Let us say I was a rock and you are a rock millions of years in the past. we are communicating with each other I could have said one day we might be able to walk and speak. with each other by sound coming from a hole in our head

I say to you as a rock that we will be able to do anything we would like. you called me an idiot and killed me now do you see I was right will you kill me again? come together I will still try to be a common friend among those who live. Finally, every one of you each as one person have the key to everything known to mankind.

Chapter 2

Let's say your name is Zonia you need help finding out something, let's say how to grow a pumpkin. in relation to yourself owning thousands upon thousands of seeds. you have no idea how to grow them, you ask a dear loved one named ZACHA five thousand feet away in a house. you walk through grass, mud also creeks.

the question is brought to light about so call help with growing a field of pumpkins. says she has been wanting to find pumpkin seeds yet only does she know they need to be put in the ground. now you both have helped each other with a touch of knowledge.

Zacha plus zone is now outside digging up the soil planting the seeds. After planting five hundred seeds the pair watch and wait for seven days. On the seventh day Zecha screams "now you have wasted my time also broken my trust". -thee loved one thinks you have tricked her with bad seeds-

with this you get angry with these words and say your thoughts to the loved one. "You have spoken lies you never knew how to grow pumpkins you are worthless ". there is conflict in between the two of you do you see how anger is irrelevant to life. ABE is walking past with a staff having a good day when he heard a commotion over the hill.

I walk up and see two people fighting. I asked why are you both mad at each other? they blame it on one another and tell me why they are upset. I tell them to calm down also that I have a solution so preceded to walk over to a pond. I fill a vase to the brim with cold *water, I soaked all the holes.*

after three days I returned to see the seeds beginning to sprout. the two humans are best friends again, not upset with each other anymore. In the case of them finding out the one they cared for was not lying nor was trickery involved. I then depart for seventy-seven days.

After my short quest of pure knowledge, I come back to see that all these plants have produce pumpkins. The pair let me know they are more than happy for my help. Thus, that I may keep a pumpkin you hand me perfect plump orange one. I intentionally smashed it on the ground telling each, that you would blame one another after excepting the task.

In that, they would scream and hurt one another they are supposed to love and take care of. "They should think about why they excepted the help of each other morally". not for the reason of a pumpkin yet because they have been through so much together. when Zecha and zone witnessed me smash the pumpkin, they now have turned the hatred from one another towards ABE. I was almost killed for a pumpkin; a large Rock was thrown at me striking me in the head.

 I stood up and I walked toward the heart of existence leading me from danger of the blind. zone had said they started the pumpkins together and never needed my help. yet as you can see, the words which could have torn them apart have only made me stronger. also, by using the brain I was gifted, their bond is unbreakable. now alone from all blind I may see the most beautiful and mysterious thing known to man the sunlight.

The sun is like a heartbeat to us if the heart gives out so does everything on Earth. for instance, if every plant will eventually die off for the reason of no carbon dioxide from the Sun. with all plant's dead, all animals including humans will perish with the sun. furthermore, if All of the universe's elements come together in such a perfect manner.

To create humans, one distant offspring of good and evil will not only be on both sides. yet he will be able to soak up all evil and project it in such a way. to change a bad thinking person into one who can overcome all thy neighbors. this little change will open minds of all who have even a shred of good left inside of them.

One will come to see, he/she has the ability to help the devil's worshiper change their mind. by being a strong person not in their heart yet tangled and tied inside their brain. not waking up every morning to do what they love (or hate) for themselves. nonetheless doing what they love only in the case of loving you.

that person would learn to do what they loved. after the start of the job only hating it for the reason or wanting to rather be with you. also, this is why they would start to love the job they always remembering you. this is the reason there is too many conflicts, one that is being worked for may say something about bills.

which the hate is not intended toward the human, it is consumed this way. each is not initially angry at their loved one when they are fighting. the government and economy have treated them this way, one does not feel things will get better. if both would sit down and figure out the easiest solution for food, water all bills will be solved.

the bond will be untouchable all will see, nothing in the universe could separate this. there are some things in the universe that will stay far from it. this is a perfected relationship also will show the universe something they would like to have. as well this relationship will create more and more love, showing all mankind impossible is right in front of them.

they will only get to own this if Fate has this in store for their change of mind. your change of mind will be acceptable to the force must consist of many outcomes. regret in a way is wishing you never had done something, not wanting to do this so-called item

Again. by knowing you shouldn't do it, knowing right from wrong, also change of the mind.

you living the way you think you should from the day of being born following yourself. just because someone has treated you with love from the beginning of your life. does not mean in any way possible that you should follow the way they treat others. Let me speak of the Sun the Moon and the Earth.

the Suns fire helps us live also be able to see the moon at night. the Moon is somewhat dead as far as I heard with no life. yet by the fire of the sun, it will be alive at night we will only see at night. when we are supposed to be asleep now with this perfect order all three are indeed alive.

for me seeing the moon at night shows me something has ended its work for my rest. rest for all of life on the planet as well this is very nice to think about. also, the moon lit up shows me the sun is still alive. every time I see it has moved; I know it will surely come back around for me to see. the night and day make me think of good and bad scenarios. where in the sun will be God's time, in the night is the devil's work. the devil in the mind did not create anything except creating humans' punishment.

by the sun shining on the moon also make me feel like there is something watching all of us. as if the plan is always protected for eternity rather one believes it or not it will be seen. light in the dark is good dark in the light is bad many meanings to this. For safety or just for all to have relief this keeps me calm either way.

one can say I am starting to feel as if the force would like us to finish the plan. by ourselves on the blind side of a neighbor we are weak like a twig in the ocean. yet All shall be powerful by enlightenment together the devil in the mind will forever disappear. (an object in motion tends to stay in motion unless acted upon by a greater force) - Sir Isaac Newton.

my thoughts on this are overwhelming my first thoughts is my body will stay in motion. In the case of taking a certain opposite Force out of the way. In doing this many amazing things would happen like speaking evil to someone could result in violence today. the opposite force will need to be taking out so violence will still indeed be there to see. it would just be the grass we walk on top of (hint) by it staying in motion.

things are not really good things also bad things are not really bad things. I only will say this for the truth of not being able to keep it for eternity. you being born is irrelevant if you are to die and lose it all you have gained.

which means all gathered in your life will disappear, how can one other than me wish to accept death? accepting a kid to die is a terrible thing to have to comprehend for anyone. why is it a neighbor will not even try to stop that from happening? even if all hope is lost, at least I was there fighting. I was there to get embarrassed, to show all I was not an idiot.

furthermore, the real reason why I choose to do the plan is I will not sit and do nothing. watching horrible situations, bad words also treacherous actions even death has changed my mind about greed neighbored by power. I've been on this path my entire life I will not surrender to devilish ways. I will surrender all bad habits in order to See real Joy from someone honest.

Love also relationships will prosper on thee never ending golden path. what it is, you see now is what you think is true love or honest relationships. you will all see in time dust does not lie and for the dust in your palm. This was formed for you to have a gift you chose to factor it into an object which is okay.

do not disrespect this gift or you will also be the dust in someone else's Palm. have you heard the saying "the best things in life are usually what kills us". this is a very true in many ways if I was to work my entire life. so, I could keep my family alive blood or not they all still was made like myself.

let's say I worked for 30 years at a factory so I could keep my family alive. I feel that I'm doing all I can yet I am only keeping them on the track to death. without knowing it you are following the path of everyone who has died in the past. all will except using the knowledge of past ancestors they have cared about.

The words will be entangled in their brain which will inevitably end all joy also pain. yet create fake joy and fake pain for anyone still left standing on Earth. if you follow the heard, the heard will not hate you nor will they think differently of you. in the reason of happiness that they are on the right path seen you are following them.

This will set relief in their life feeling as if all will stay the same. After a loved one passes away, they will ask others and themselves why this has happened. why do I need to kill myself physically blind man's work I have done this yes, I don't want anyone doing it. why shall I have to work for what they need to die happily I would rather not loose anyone.

I have been a slave with my brain for five years to keep you all alive. with you alive you should not care for others and how they keep making fun of you. what they will think formed from dust shall a neighbor be that dust this is the path of overpower. they enjoyed using a word as a sword thrust shall a sword come back at them.

I will be calm for those who have died, I will fight for the living who are calm. The calm has been waiting I will kneel for those who cannot speak nor stand. I will only finish the plan with the knowledge of knowing it has to be complete.

not for me, not for anyone particularly, it is already planned this I will finish. I will except being last only in the case of learning the actions of all in front. Watching and soaking it all up I will be most knowledgeable of good and evil out of all who live.

even the person second to last will think he has it better than the person in front. The person first in line has the choice to walk beside everyone or to be a car. second-to-last will never know anyone is behind him if not side by side with the leader. to be born and not helping anyone is the same as not being born.

To be on earth and not give life to one rather it be a basket of bread or actually saving someone physically. can be worth more than stopping someone from doing harm in many ways you will see. now by me giving life to someone in the case of giving life to their brain life of knowledge. never understood in recent times each word is written by the string of pictures only few will understand.

an enemy from the day before may seem nice in front of you. Yet one has planned intentions from the past, you do not want to be a part of this. it's very hard to give all this up knowing you missed a good time. It is worth more to keep what you've never had, locked away then to lose what you wanted in reality.

life will always be a masterpiece in the eye of someone who has fully respected the gift. to what creator there is no flaw you may think there is yet that is the path you have chosen. for this you will get to a dead end on the right path there is no end. With my observation when I am accompanied by a fellow human, I tend to notice we are complete opposites.

yet when I see them with others, they seem compatible with each other. me and doing the plan that seems so impossible I will only focus on this. for now, until the day comes, I will proceed to go on with letting humans think they are right. the evil they continue to do in life is a reason I am doing this.

in the case of me always being told I was wrong, writing a profound amount of the plan. now I'm speaking of not bothering them in any way possible by the procedure I continue to carry out. Many will speak dust upon my head also throw invisible fire towards me. I will flood myself with the coolest water which will calm my blood.

only in the reason of being boiled by your fire sent to harm me. The water will also cleanse my skin washing every particle of Dust Away spoken on my scalp. I will be dry of all immoral actions brought to my life with the assistance of my neighbor. I will never bring the same sword thrust against he has done to me.

also, whomever is the creator of these actions against me must know it is usually not intentional. It is how they been taught also how they learned by people they care about or even someone they would not talk to. they may forget where the knowledge was giving rather it be good or evil. It is understandable so I will Neal to them in return of this hatred.in order to save the next person to cross the path of this same situation.

he that cuts my heart open in front of all to see has been murdered mentally. He was shown true hatred and treacherous Settings, you must love him more than anyone. They might not have gotten life worse than you yet they took it a lot. Yee, do they know who you are their words false or not, shall open doors never expected to have been existed.

they need to follow the path no one will think twice about taking. kneel on one knee when approached by any human or non-human you will know when to get on both knees. listening also actually understand these words can hurt the feelings of many people close to me. I honestly wish they would help me finish the plan rather than burning it with the dust from a tree.

often much of humanity will block out my words by glancing at me like I am just an opinion. if my words were to actually be taken seriously you would Be saddened. you throw my words in the garbage with no remorse, then you will ask why the earth is so terrible. what you asked for many times, the only hope given to you for your needs is in the trash.

the possibility of you getting what you desire is now to a minimum. the tools needed to save you have been in front of you, while instead of using these tools. you did not want to build your needs; all have asked many times for it to be built for them. why is that all will ask for something when you can go get it. or in the case of asking to stop doing something or for an item to stop you can stop it yourself. I'm speaking of objects not of Health for you and or a dear loved one.

In one who may see the sunlight and all who breathe will soon lose this Feeling. if they continue to not help me keep what I do not own the nobody will own or love anything. Myself Is nothing of anything I am alive so shall I live if I have spoken evil shall I not wake tomorrow. I will not utter words of a fool unless I will have to speak to a foolish human.

These words are not only being written, yet being spoken with intentions for one other than myself to understand. on September 5th 2021 I acted alone on smashing 8 store windows 5 different operations of the government. have been damaged to my clear perception in reality. in many Minds across earth will this be seen as destructive.

however, would you rather listen to a broken piece of glass or someone who said he smashed the windows. to see if the owner would care for a fellow human or an object is all that was meant by my actions.   the more you work or try to keep someone alive the hardest it is when you lose it right in front of you. This is the objective I've been fighting for so you will not go through this.

it's not that I was not thinking on my birthday, it's that I was thinking too much. My birthday will not mean anything if I can't spend my next one with someone who will not be here. now to stand by and to watch someone you care for very much on drugs. I drug will alter your life and brain to where you are not yourself anymore. it was made to kill love and also for those who are evil to change into

. to think of what is not needed for them to live life peacefully on earth. with no desires or urges for anything that was not given the day they were born. drugs were taking advantage of, only was they meant for health and to feel better in their mind.

not to use to feel better from not doing drugs, for this you will see the ultimate fate. For the reason of taking advantage of something, shall your brain be used by the drug as well. if an individual was to ignore all around them (all) "meaning anything. in which a neighbor has died for died because of or died without".

you will see all those who have killed another for an object or a need one will actually save their own life also my neighbor. all in your life will be peaceful including intelligent you will also be respected. by those who have done this evil or seen evil, this will save you. it will pass through each across the Earth like a pandemic "virus", disease.

One will be surprised with the faith on top of wisdom you all will be filled with. over the time of this treacherous Journey the task I have chosen to take on, started to rip me apart. only in the reason of each person doing their job by cutting down the apple tree to buy an Apple.

I only say this because when you do not listen to someone who says they can help you more than you will ever know. you will continue to do blind work for example a doctor will listening to himself save a life yet he does not realize he is only delaying the person's time of death .as for when I said cutting down an apple tree to buy an apple or feed the family.

by me doing my job to make the doctor listen I will lose everyone on Earth for the rest of Eternity. if for some reason I can persuade one person alive of a beautiful Miracle of a plan. all who live on earth just one person will spread the knowledge to Thy Neighbor. this may indeed save their life and or all of their neighbors my entire life would not be wasted.

I am now standing in the Moonlight knowing it is either a gift or something sinister. I will only get to conclude my thoughts if I will not only hold my rock for eternity. yet get to dissect it to determine what it is I am dealing with. by doing so I will know more than ever imagined I will only get to consume this knowledge.

if for some many souls will be able to understand my words. Also to look deeper into the line of unethical Journey's which one who is blind will turn into dust for having being curious. for the blind one will only see the water flowing in the creek also knowing each fish. Those who flock their power Above All Around will miss the ability of creating new fish.

never seen by humans on Earth nor the ability to reincarnate fish from beyond the dead. not only will you be able to see how over powering a neighbor is irrelevant to his vision. he will help one see past being powerful also to see the point of time when one's eyesight by the ancestors was created. all items in the sight of the ancestors past present and future will come to light.

as the Rock from the tallest mountain has chipped away in seconds. Will Row breaking into smaller pieces on its journey to a long-time resting spot. in time you will see reversing this affect will alter all of your thoughts in many ways.

this will show you each item one will stumble upon can be broken down. into the very first material of what started you reversing the outcome of the object nor human you see now it can be built up into a sight that will blind the sun. by knowing this starting material, (present of Life) knowledge will fill you. knowing this will help you from ending the start of your conscience.

in short, I will say by finding the beginning of one path you will ultimately reach the end. which in this case the end of one thing is also the beginning to never-ending knowledge.it will be the end of not knowing and thee beginning to a world which was originally giving. you will stop one from doing a good promise, by your evil in the mind which is blinding

You.

by believing he is doing evil you have not only killed him you've killed yourself you also killed everyone living. Consequences are coming upon you, for this is the worst evil that has formed upon the grounds of Earth. For an explanation you will believe the staff I walk with has been stolen from you or someone you care for. by spreading this evil upon my name, you are committing a crime which I see is acceptable with death.

I will not condone this nor will I accept one doing either opposite of each product given in the subject. each is irrelevant and is not given permission to do so above a subject's head. for he has been listened to by someone who is not you nor me. he has been thrown into a lake of fire with your thought processes you have watched him burn.

knowing you are dry and pristine in health; this power is leading you where you belong. the Dust when you have walked on are now walking upon your corpse. a person that may do you wrong over and over again may not mean to do it intentionally. or they may be trying to save the soul of one who is loved more by you. how they will treat you may actually be killing them more than you will ever know. by you both falling into a pit of not knowing, one Prestige knowledge is that you will be wrong, be right, be even. to be wrong is to give power to the one who is blind, to be right is to give power to yourself. which you would be blind as well you can still be tied to a light.

To be even is to let them understand you know how they can be thinking this way. yet letting them see you are appreciative of their thoughts and telling them your side. now for being even you will bring one closer rather than pulling yourself away nor throwing them away. this I will call splitting the river for this is how you will see two will always come to one.   Also, one will always go unto two if you are even 50/50 you will see all different paths.

all are connected even though they will eventually spread apart they only can for growing together. become separate yet together Down for blinding on you will be the clog in the river with this will ruin how the Holy Spirit Will Flow. by doing this blind decision you will dry out if so of yourself also the body of the one you will have blinded this will in life where ones was not a site of any in the past .

you will often say that you will trust the force which has given your life the second you are to look down so you can make sure you do not step into the unknown fate that is where you break the trust of the force who guides you from harm for this your ankles will be untrustworthy to thy grass and shall the water you trust burn your feet . let me explain the select subject if you was giving a birthday present you may think you have gotten what it is you have been wanting or have been asking someone for" from whoever it may be and whatever it may be what it is that you was giving is now yours to do with what it is that you please I think about this one very critically if I say ABE was given the gift of life. should I hurt the feelings of whomever it shall be by either taking advantage of this gift for greed power or having fun(what the gift was not meant for) or knowing what it is I should do and not accepting the gift at all but this is my choice to decide to complete this task rather I be wrong is irrelevant .

so, if I was to say I will root for both teams I am wrong yet right either way. I will never loose myself also for someone who has fully won. will not be able to use the power of knowing I lost against me nor will I see a dear neighbor cry. thinking they lost to me for this way I both failed also had a victory. it indeed takes three to be one I wept with my neighbor I also cheered with my brother. Saying that I am wrong about all of these writings now and coming to find out I was wrong. This would mean I won also I failed it does mean anything at all. if I had informed you, I was wrong before proceeding with the plan and ending up truly speed balling. I indeed won in my own mind by knowing I had the intentions to fail by trying to succeed. by these common ways of Thinking you will come to find out you are meant to live for eternity.

if the one you are teaching interprets you to either correct you or tell you you are wrong. they are not using your words wisely nor are they listening to . Their brain is full of fire causing pure confusion this it will be dried up with no rain. Which means one has Involved their mind in an irrelevant Journey for the mind of the devilish ways. "You are powerful you are always knowing more than anyone alive rather.

You being wrong is irrelevant knowing your words Are killing your friend while lifting you higher. You shall lose your rock shall it also turn into dust" purposely towards an evil mind. Just because you will stumble upon something once does not mean that you will have the same experience again.

also having experienced once why do you think the experience will not happen again the same as before. as you have seen before, will be seen again seen before will be seen again. now have seen before it will only be shown this one time. or to never have seen or been through an experience you will never know it exists. if knowing something exists also never experiencing the presence of contact with a different situation or reality.

knowing it is there thought of how you know a different reality is there to be seen. if not have falling into this opposite side for it never happening in the past It shall never happen. for it never happening in the past it will start and happen for eternity for even reading my words one will see it is happening at this second .to show you also it has always happened in the past it will never stop happening. furthermore, it has always happened in the past it will come to an abrupt ending. you will see all is true, every day will have its appropriate ending. every ending in a night will have ultimately started from a beginning. you may say is a lie, you will get power all who hold their Rock, will see your wickedness. I will give you a short passage I have stumbled upon months ago when walking I inevitably had to pause. good along with evil go perfect together in the case of doing a task known impossible. if good and evil love their life and choose to keep it they both. will have to take refuge in the opposite side that they do not live.

by this I should not have to speak or nor give an explanation for you know where you stand. the destruction you have created has done its deed are you truly happy with the path you have chosen. just because you have been noticed by many and loved by all among your side. for the Unholy power that does nothing to prove you will be around to enjoy this disloyalty. to your life you will never see this until you misplace your rock.

When misplacing your rock, you will see your heart is the one to choose when your time has come. the heart is connected with a force which is greater than what it has created. I will explain further I am planting a garden which are living organisms as of me as well. if the seed I was to plant was stuck between two rocks this particular seed. will eventually be destroyed it will be away from what it needs. The wind may come from the farthest thought from you as a helping hand. thy rain may grow the roots if close to the soil it may make it to a real life. that wind will sweep the seed to where it needs to be when this plant is grown to the point to bring you oxygen. this will prove to everyone they are not needed for the start of life. by this being true does not mean you was not given life to figure out how to keep this plant alive.

rain, sun, animals also soil to all come together for you to live. means you should give back something as well for it gives to you it would only be right. your actions and abuse of hate towards a brother or sister will ultimately mean nothing in time. for your heart gets weaker every second you are here on Earth. for reasons which Are only coming to light in this book I write in relation for me to have knowledge. which one has stolen I am starting to feel as if I should not share this knowledge.

Among all who walk upon the Earth however it was given to myself. either way in relation that I was not alive thousands of years ago when the Bible was formed. I feel as if some passages of the Bible May refer to 1 in a specific way. speaking of something I have found or doing you shall not come to conclusions just yet. I will follow the one created my life rather you hate me is relevant to anyone dead or alive. I will stand for the dead and I will walk away from the living. the reason I will do this is the dead cannot listen the dead cannot see. Now thee living choose to not listen and choose to not see. this will not help me by that they choose to only help themselves. I have coped with the fact that I will perish this is why I will write this book. not for any on Earth to feel bad nor be angry with me for not working harder at finishing the plan. as what I do will be done for what will not be done shall never seek daylight in my eyes.

I have been here peacefully for many minutes as I noticed something on my arm. I had not glanced at this creature nor did I think this was a harmful animal. in many different occasions would I jerk my hand or Flinch not this time. I slowly raise my arm up to the presence of a dear companion many have the name as a praying mantis. A very gentle creature, I slowly gave him /her flight to the top of my staff. standing up against this table in the calmness of night little did I know. a nelson County Sheriff was about 20 ft away watching me as this pure soul ascended to the top of my staff. the cruiser Was turned on, he drove beside me asking how are you ABE.

I started to focus on the book the praying mantis is still at the top of my staff keeping me company as I had put the word company, he / she then takes off for if you say I have formed this story from dust then shall your life be that dust. what is very interesting about this story is the other night when I was writing. I had come across something I had not recognized, written months before in a smaller note pad. it said "if you will speak the truth of thee staff it will be a lie soon after you shall see".

the line in which I said the praying mantis was still on top of my staff keeping me company. right after I wrote this word (company) it took off actually in the middle of writing the word. since I was not done writing the word yes it was indeed considered a lie. this Is very important to understand a human with sight may see a second sun before all else. I do see I am on the right path and am very pleased to see these amazing Scenes of unnoticed Treasures. you will tell me I cannot led you astray from your beliefs you only say this for power. when all I have done is to explain why your beliefs have been misused by yourself and many others.

I have witnessed all, disrespect the name of thee whom would kneel for. you tell all you love who created your life yet I see regret in your eyes. standing in front of a crowd of neighbors you bend down to praise a statue of thy Creator. all neighbors respect you for doing so yet, those who do not like you make fun of you. One only speaks to those who respects you the very next day you are told by whom.   you know are good that the creator has given instructions for all to praise a statue down the road. of someone who saved your life you listen to these false words by accepting these orders. now that you have listened to the words from a lying spirit those who respect you.

*   also, those who do not like you will be parting ways, do you know these words are from the creator. yet you listen with your ears not your eyes do not listen to the words of the powerful soul. for he will lead you to your death listen to the sound of a rock falling and hitting the ground.*

*   this will give light too many words this will save many humans if they will listen to a rock. humans who have never listened to a rock would talk drama*

in the case of arguments. I took off on a walk away from rash words between neighbors knowing it's best.   For me not to consume this in my life it was thunder storming everywhere floodwaters were on my mind. as well I had not been touched by the smallest raindrop, I get to a patch of freshly cut grass. to my surprise it was dry I Surely partook resting in this area.

I looked up It was clear also that the storm was in A Perfect Circle all around me. The lightning and thunder rolled around me, the bright stars were easily seen by my vision. this was appreciated by myself I would call this a pre-calculated experience.

*   it was proven to me I was on the right path by walking away from self-harm. "Self-harm" in the case of ones who are color-blind having intentions for power over a brother or sister .by me leaving I was given peace in the scariest storm. If myself knows all the wrong answers I can help you find the answer you need.   to find the answer is accepting what happens good or bad past and future. Looking to find an answer means you know*

your strong to what you stumble upon. reading this book also means that what was given in the past was not suitable for your mind in some way, an answer is upon yourself. the words from the mind of a foolish human will occupy the minds of the highest wisdom.

this will change the minds of who you have turned to stone and who you have turned to liquid. this will stick to the dust of Earth for all of eternity like a Fossil. when I happen to come across a rock on the ground many people say it is a fossil. that is seen in a confused mind childlike one will not think it is yourself.

you will say it's a fossil not even thinking of it being a Rock. if I can pick up a rock and bring it to Life by touching it like it having thoughts, walk and talk. if this rock can do all these amazing things as you, that rock can live for eternity. If the rock could do all of these things for even one second.

also, Eternity would happen as fast as you dropping a rock the sound it produces is as quick if you blinked. I had a wonderful friend long ago my friend was right beside me; he had not eaten food for 13 days. in the case of being poor, he was also depressed his family had recently died.

I had stumbled upon him on my walk he asked me for some of the food that I had. keep in mind I have a wagon of food I tell him "I will not give you any at all". I sat with him for 24 hours until he passes away, after his death I opened his mouth.

I put some Mana Softly on his tongue "would you call this murder"? I can tell you why it is I also can't tell you why it is not. the mana was poisoned it was bad and could not be eaten by no one.

it would have killed my friend I was also poor I had no food. why it is murder the Manna could have actually saved him long enough to get him real food. I honestly do not like humans at all I've been done Dirty by all who walk on earth.

I have seen different strands of hate or accusations from both sides of Good and Evil. nor am I surprised in the case of knowing where I stand, I will stand above both good and bad people. Most I've met are blind which makes them a loose end this can be devastating for all who breath.

they wanted to use power against me even though I am doing this plan to help them all. By stopping what it is they do not want to see it is not seen by anyone what I am doing this for. it is best for Earth that I might as well suffer for all who have perished on Earth nor any Planet.

all has happened for blind power over one who listens to a rock. a blind person will be the one who thinks he has power by throwing the Rock. now the one who listens to the Rock will know what all could be done with the rock. Any and everything about The Rock, he who does this will become a rock in the mind. to become a rock is to be presently conscience with all your surroundings. to know each possible outcome of a tree's life also a pebbles life.

this will fill your brain with pure knowledge with whatever you will see or know in a thousand years. this is why many who love nor hate you soul will try to overpower you. in relation to them having no clue what you could be capable of with the knowledge you hold.

indeed, could you explode the entire

universe or create any life yet you could make one delay death. Also keeping their body alive for eternity our ancestors have done themselves also their offspring deadly Wrong. by not listening to something or someone, if you choose to follow in the footsteps. Shall you see you are powerless against the knowledge you think you own.

the sound of a rock dropping is the sound of all knowledge at your fingertips. yet the only way you can get the knowledge is to be giving it in the right circumstances. starting from the beginning of time I do not know if any of you have been given the Divine knowledge. yet those who will stumble upon it will be stronger than all who walk.

certain circumstances had to have happened in a perfect sequence, they also can be endless. I can never stop naming situations that could happen for one to be a rock in the mind. it would not be concluded for eternity unless each human alive could find this knowledge.

Each alive would be on track never to be lost nor found, not hold it nor toss it away. its presence will be in time, the plan would then be done for our world be perfect. with all who do not want Power, this is good show those with power that it is irrelevant to life. in many ways you are not God do not try and be powerful over another human for neither is he.

one will flip over a leaf that has fallen and see one side is lighter colored then the other side. This knowledge is needed that one leaf may show you a path you should take in life. I choose to mix both colors together to be both opposites in order to save a leaf from dying. It is your job to soke up all bad and good intentions from thy neighbor's.

no matter how much pain you endure you will have to lead all the blind. You will be at peace to overcome those who will overpower one another. I do not feel that calling a human a name in the form of a joke is for us to do. or to curse at someone with evil intentions these both have no meaning to me I will look past them.

Tell thee blind, the truth, that you love them then walk away you may need to fight. yet only in the presence of an altercation, will you need to do this.

this could make all blind, even more Angry it honestly is the best way to do. it is as dangerous for you as it would be to get angry yourself.

if yourself knows for a fact you are in the right you need to remember to stay calm in front of all who are angry. with me continuing on my own path this may Save my soul more than it would if I explained myself. path if they feel I am trying to overpower them I will Sadly be killed .in the case of move him believing is right and following a human who has been followed.

this could also blind me, thinking something that is not true. it could very well be the death of my life is why I will try and finish this book. in case, I am killed in front of an evil person all will see they only killed a helping hand.

I was approached by a human who enjoyed his peers and women seeing him as tough. I only was hungry I meant no harm towards him or anyone around him he walked up to me. calling me names making fun for all to see I turned around and said that I love him very much. that I loved all around him he wanted to know why I had smashed all the windows in New Haven.

I said that it was only for a reason of my peers being rude also humas disrespecting the gift of life. he said with anger and it's because you're a piece of rubbish He then struck me in the nose. I lifted up the staff my Creator had given to me and I'm bluntly hit him with it. My staff Shirley was broken I then punched him as he done to me.

as I was not safe, my friends came to stop him I ended up getting up off the pavement. speaking with a tone from Pure knowledge you are dust all of you watching are nothing but dust. and none deserve life Yee I dearly love each and every one of you. I then was giving my belongings such as my book which had fallen from my .

I walked home this night with nothing but flooded with appreciation of my dear Creator. I was happy with all the confidence I was given and standing in front of evil with a blind mind. Not too long after a few days in the future when making copies of my book at the library.

I was on my walk home when a black truck

stopped and proceeded speak to me. why I was walking, my name, I told him he said have a good night, to stay off the road. this is a sign of power knowing I was already in the grass. later on in the night I lay awake figuring I would take a stroll under the moon.

I was maybe thirty minutes in when I noticed the exact truck pull into a driveway. the same man told me I was in his uncle's yard I reminded him he had said to stay off the road. I was only doing as he said, he then drove away upset his power was no use to knowledge.

he was angry and called the cops telling lies about me about 8 cops showed up at my house. angry with me I told them all I loved them it made them even more mad. I got a wave of cuss words only for walking, all of them then drove off.

I am on the right path knowing I am cursed by dealing with the blind mind. you see I have lost my friend the way that was worse for us both. yet this situation we went opposite ways calmly and on our own priorities. the reason that condemned us both was soft on our minds though was rough on our feet.

if I had chosen to feed Darkness, I would have lost not only my friend but also myself. I would not have walked above ground not seen light what was given to me that is what I have. anything I do not have is irrelevant also is pointless for me to kill myself trying to get.

if I have seen others in past experiences grab this darkness that I turned away from. also watching them suffer from Thorns leaving trails of blood. I will follow the trail to the corporate of what caused such pain and suffering.

this should help shine light on what it is that has led to my dear friend getting condemned. let's say I need to feed myself with food first I would have to fix Me up a tool. to catch a fish after doing so I would need what Many would call bait worms to lure in the fish.

for me to lift up a rock, stone to find worms the first Brick I pulled up has no worms. instead of me giving up on this most people among Earth would lift up a second Stone. to push Faith most likely they would find them fate however this example is for good purposes.

you may see bad intentions in killing an animal for yourself yet your ancestors had to delay death. to create your life, you do not have to follow as they have done yet you should respect this. to give you an opportunity to choose a different food source they did not have the choice.

to think of a human's perspective, if a fellow neighbor chooses to turn away from each, Stone by stone

. "Food source" they went from turning away from worms' fish, Deer and also eggs. he has had enough of these also ate these for so long and disrespects the taste of all.

so, he turns to you, he desires forbidden blood only in the case of it being an equal species. he should cut off his own arm and feast if he wants forbidden blood. you have accepted what it is you was given you enjoyed the same taste a million times. you do not look for more taste why should you be a taste to a deceiver of life.

my friend and doing as she pleased and myself being an empty Rock with no bait. she looks for more to fill her wishes and desires so once she gets the taste of what she wants. she will never be happy; this is the end for the taste of her wishes. forbidden blood shall taint her mouth and it be glued shut she shall not taste again.

for evil will kill itself off it is blind to all now let's say my dear friend had lifted every single Stone. also turn away from everything there is to eat because she had never tasted true good. true love because of other deceivers which had ate from her she sadly could be drowning herself as we speak.

unless what I have done to not want or need the taste of it will fill her life. with one taste, the taste of Life the taste of Victory and the taste of pure love. to be one if this shall fall to her palm then you both will overcome all good and evil. you both shall live and thrive and it will destroy all who will try and trample you.

Chapter 3

Clunk "pop' clunk pop "my eyes opened with blurred vision I was looking at a tree dropping apples. at the time I had no idea what I was looking at, only in the reason of awakening for the first time in my life. I was astounded by the sight I did not know what I was, nor did I know anything but my self-existed. I stood up and saw I was on top of a cliff with fascinating colors all around and under me.

I saw leaf's falling with the apples, keep in mind it is the beginning of time so words were not to my knowledge. I focused on the large tree for a moment when a strange animal appears on the side of a limb. it had long arms and short legs the hair was like mine yet it was blueish in color like the sky, I was not frightened. Figuring it was a companion "picking up an apple I busted it on the tree.

not knowing what I was doing the animal climbed down fast grabbing it out of my hand. Holding up a piece of it in the air towards me putting it in his mouth and taking a bite. Furthermore, handing me a piece I figured he also meant for me to try it. I did so and I had a sensation of sweetness fill my tongue as if the apple was put on the cliff for us to enjoy.

After a while I was curious of a dark spot behind the tree, I pointed to it and the animal point to the sky. I looked at the direction and was instantly blinded everything was dark, to my knowledge now I figured I looked upon it too quickly. I fell to the dirt screaming "my eyes were burning with fire "nothing was seen except for darkness. I felt the creatures grasp on my chin holding up my head then pushing my eye lids closed.

I heard another sound it was a voice "YOU MUST NOT LOOK AT THE FIRE IN A RUSH DO NOT BE SO CURIOUS". I don't know why it is I could understand the voice but it flowed like water the way I can describe it now is that it was like thunder. I felt that I was being taught, I was not worried or scared, for this is my first encounter with God. I felt a rush of air fill my eyes they were cool and even, the darkness slowly washed away.

I started to slowly see light again I then could see the animal by my side he again pointed to the sky. I did not look, so I pointed to myself my entire body then start to vibrate. something came out of my body and I watched it shoot into the clouds 7 heart beats later I watched my wife levitate down to me. with the same length hair as me and the animal yet she looked kind of different then us in a way.

As she descended and landed upon the dirt, she spoke I will teach you words pointing to her own mouth. I understood what she was saying yet I still could not speak "I did not know how". then I hear the same thunderous voice once more A PEICE OF YOU IS NOW GOING TO HELP TEACH YOU, MY CHILD. I GIFT TO YOU A LIFE WITH FAMILY I GIFT TO YOUR SPOUSE SOME OF MY KNOWLEDGE.

YEE TO THE BOTH OF YOU TO EAT THE FRUIT OF KNOWLEDGE IT IS your everlasting heart and is NOT TO EVEN BE TOUCHED. "The clouds dissipated and he left" I indeed was amazed by what has happened the animal was still eating an apple in a bush. the girl looked at me and said I'm going to teach you some words she picks up a stick. And draws an AB in the dirt with a line in the middle and says that is you then she draws C V in the dirt with a line through it and says that is me.

Now that I am older, I see that B is man that came out of the ground because the A is up. And I see that C is woman that came from the sky because V is pointed down. she called me A and I called her E after I was taught the letters and symbols words came very easy to me. She taught me how to count with rocks laying them out in different columns so I would learn quickly.

As I did, she would reward me with fruit like some of what we have today kind of like strawberries and grapes. Most of which are the same as back then yet some will be recreated in the near future. thee animal we referred to as Columbia he was very intelligent by his own knowledge .as for things he would learn all by himself he could climb trees "peal fruit "what fruit was poisonous and not healthy for us also could he learn many words.

We had a cave under the cliff we all would climb down too to sleep in and live it was home for us and we enjoyed life. until the day the animal was out picking fruit, he came across a tree with blueish red bumpy and smooth pears. he grabbed one and brought it back to the cave giving it to CV she grabbed it. And say it looked very good I remember like it was today she asked her what it was.

Columbia spoke about a ground animal saying it was the lord's fruit and it was put here for us to enjoy. She picked it up and threw the fruit down the hill saying it must be the fruit god forbid us to eat. Columbia got sad by this action of hers he goes away to the garden to draw on rocks. I told CV that Columbia was sad she should go speak with him she agrees and hurries off.

She said to me later on that she got up there and he was speaking to a long laying down animal. she introduced herself and Columbia runs away to leave them alone the animal says to her why will you not eat the lord's fruit? she said to him the lord spoke about us not eating that fruit, for it is forbidden. The animal says why did her put it here for you to see if you cannot eat it.

She told the animal that he is right and proceeds to eat walk down to the fruit of knowledge and takes a bite from it. Then she starts to feel different in a way she starts to look at the animal from a different perspective as he laughs. AB came to the garden and sees CV saying what have you done. you have turned from God he says not to eat that fruit CV told me that it is what makes everyone happy if I eat it.

AB: that may be true yet they did not give your life they are just in it

CVS starts to cry as AB pick up the fruit and takes a bite as well and says you will not be the only one.

who has forsaken him I will be beside you as you are a piece of me, I will take the punishment with you. I remember the taste so clearly the shell of it was hard on the outside yet the inside was mush and felt impact on itself. the inside was purple the taste was sweet like a pear though it was strong like a lemon.

I could hear my eyes shut when I blinked, I could also taste the clear air, everything was different for the rest of my life. I looked at CV and she was beautiful like a sunset I did not see her as myself anymore I seen her as a piece of God. yet I knew this was not true or she would not have turned against him. I also seen her as an evil being on most days like a weak branch that cannot handle hatred from others.

like she would rather hurt one that should not be taken advantage of. now myself I felt saddened by my actions as well though on a different level than CV. after a few weeks of trying to build a shelter with CV and Columbia. CV falls out of a tree landing on both of her arms snapping them both.

Her screams are heard by God and clouds form yet again in the sky a hand comes down and swoops her up. Setting her down back on her feet after he seen us wearing leaves and vines as clothes. He speaks I have healed your other half yet I see you both have turned against my word. Furthermore, have ate a piece of me you did not know was not good for you.

This fruit had to be made for you to be made for it was your heart now in the case of you eating a permanent heart. you have now grown a temporary one you may feel the same now yet over time. you will grow old and parish, for this was your choice to not listen.

Now you and your other half are banished from this land. it is now covered in blood from the unworthy, shall night be yours and your children's punishment from me.

After a few days of walking with Columbia me and CV felt weird like as if we were dying. slowly was we getting weaker and weaker with every step. we sat down for a second and cv laid still I heard breathing yet she would not answer I thought she was dead. I tried shaking her and yell her name loudly yet nothing came to life I laid beside her in the darkness.

As I was awoken once more by Columbia, now I feel that when I first awoke weeks back was when I was first given life. now I feel as if I am now cursed with reliving that moment of unconsciousness for the rest of my days. maybe this is what god meant by our punishment in the night. it was very scary for me having to go through this every night after first knowing I would be unconscious at night.

I would always think about how terrible it would be to die and leave my body on earth. yet now with me back alive I am calm with my actions of the past and will not stop until the plan is finished. CV later told me she ate the fruit for love she knew something terrible would end up happening. Yet she knew it would make others happy she did not intend to hurt the feelings of God.

Nor did she know that her offspring would be affected by this decision of love. but what I have come to realize over my new time here is that true love is a powerful thing.

knowing her intentions now were not for her to be happy, it was for others to be happy "keep this in mind" All things work together for good to them that love God, to them who are the called according to his purpose: Romans 8:28.

This verse feels to me as if whatever happens in the future rather it be good or bad will eventually be a good thing or have a good outcome.

Me, CV and Columbia walked to the nearest creek after 9 days of walking and started to drink from the water it was clear. like the wind it was smooth like the top of a leaf when CV said she felt weird and unsettled. her stomach started growing very big like a giant apple it was instant. then my stomach started growing as well we both were scared on what would happen .

Yet then moments later eve is laying on the dirt when a little one comes out of her, we named him cane. it's been a few days now and my stomach started hurting I did not have a place where the baby could come through. so, me and CV agreed we would cut my stomach open to get he or she out. Columbia went and found a sharp piece of slate rock and CV started slicing through my skin straight up and down from my belly button.

I started to hear crying it was loud it was a boy. she said then came able a beautiful baby as well we wrapped him in fur like we did to cane. days passed and we found a little cave to rest in it turned into our home CV fed the cane and able with her milk. as she saw a cow doing it with her young, they grew day by day until they were old aunt to eat real food. we started to feed them fresh eggs we cooked over a fire.

Eventually cane and able were about seven years old when I was standing by a tree one day and saw the clouds get dark. the voice of God came back he spoke with knowledge yet I was calm this time. he said you have now had two of the same opposites from yours and CVs body they will have children of their own. keep them healthy for they will fix what you and CV have tried and destroyed.

I agreed with him and the clouds dissipated I told CV about the encounter with God, she said it is only right.

she said it would be a lot different if she had not eaten the fruit I agree with her as well. we never know what his plan would have been yet now after I'm alive again I do see the wonderful plan right in front of me. Every person I meet I see the pain in their eyes I see the devil in disguise only because it's the things a person is blind of.

A human being does not sit and watch rocks move in the creek on a regular basis. a human being does not see the sky stretch out like the world is getting bigger as every second passes they aren't blind by doing these things they know what they can do. by trying to pass boredom up trying to find new things to do or create new and exciting things ways of life. of trying to finish the plan. a human being says they are close to God but really are far from him.

Their once was a farm and there was a big bull named roscoe every year the cows would follow the bull. where ever he went one day the farmer took the bull and put him on a trailer. all the cows followed and got on the trailer before the farmer shut and locked the door he let the bull out. and all the cows went to the slaughter house to be killed and ate, this story goes to show, be the leader and believe in yourself. not everyone you follow will lead you to where you want to be.

.

After cane and able got to the age of 20 they both were on the mountain top giving gifts to Jehovah. Cain brought up a sack of corn, radishes, carrots and tomatoes able brought one of his fittest bulls. The offering went well but God was saddened by Cains offering in the case of that being all he had to give. he loved the offering from both of them but told him to keep the offering to feed his family. He was most joyed that he would do such a thing to help the lord Cain was hurt. only the reason that God saw how poorly he was doing in life.

Abel said to Cain "why don't you come over and ill teach you how to please God "Cain took this as if able was flocking his ability against Cain. so, when they both was home Cain went and got his favorite sword .and walked the journey to Abels hose where he was feeding the chickens. Cain the stuck him in the neck with the weapon cutting his head off.

He then put Abels body on a wagon and rode a bull up the mountain to offer God one of the best offers he could think of. when the cloud appeared God said with furry 'YOU HAVE KILLED YOUR ONLY BROTHER FOR THAT I CONDEMN YOU TO A LIFE OF WANDERING. when Cain walked back down the mountain he was met by Adam his father. Adam says to him where is your brother Cain tells him he offered him to Jehovah. because able is greedy he said Adam was furious as well and banished him from the land.

You see the power of the fruit can do deadly things also most joyful things it depends on the person. the reason why Cain killed able is jealousy brought by the fruit. If able hadn't had the fruit in him too he wouldn't have said anything like that to have him killed. that's how it works with people nowadays most people were born on Cains side.

That is why you see so much violence and hate most are born with the DNA of the fruit rather it had been Abels side or Cains. even if it wasn't a fruit in the first place the story is telling you something. let me show you my name this will make it a lot clearer to understand what I'm about to tell you.

I took my staff and shoved it through the father son and holy spirit then I see man and then woman. if you understand this then I will tell you all on earth are pieces of the lord. which means if eve came from Adam, then I am you and you are me but one is giving differences. this is why we have arguments and power over one another. because after so many humans are born the DNA from the fruit, Adam and eve are spread though out the population.

You see after the first bite of the forbidden fruit the clock started ticking for all of us. for the cause of greed and power she definitely did not receive it but her offspring did receive blind power. it is only blind because whatever we gain not outside our loved ones is going to disappear.

we fight for land that is not ours we kill for money that we cannot keep and we love those who don't deserve it.

I've peacefully waited for something to happen for the past 20 years yet what am I waiting for. When I can fix this place all by myself with the help of the mapping of course that was written by God directly .it tells me exactly what I need to do and how to do it why shall I turn away from it. this would be foolish of me not to try and finish the plan.

These things we want most in life will not always be able to be in your possession. it hurts even more to know you That you will not own it. you work for it especially knowing it's possible to keep it. when you hold something long enough it always will destroy you once you lose it.

if you get rid of it before you get to hold it and it may not hurt as bad with gods plan is a different story. with God's plan love will be seen in a different angle and it is now during the year 2023 You will kill. To keep the loved ones safe in order to protect them from evil. You will hide addictions, greed and temptations. And all other things in our human nature. You cannot control to keep that love until the day we die.

Also, will we hurt others for the reason of thinking we have everything we need? By feeling like we owned the love. Of our life. The reason why we lose all materialistic items including love. Is because we don't deserve it. The reason why we get to see what love is about is because we have to see what it's like to lose it. In order to grow. After the plan is starting. And in progress to be finished, love will not indeed. Need to be protected.

By anyone on Earth. So, none will need to kill to protect their loved ones from evil beings. For everyone Will Be held together from the light of God. None will be able to get injured or be able to die Violence can be seen, but will not be able to mean anything. It's like trying to damage water those who Are evil will be wiped off the face of the Earth. For eternity.

addiction to a substance will be gone until the sun goes out It will be able to go in your body. yet it will not affect your body Therefore, nobody will be selling drugs or be killing each other for a substance. Or nor will they die because of a substance every overdose Death Will be at a 0. Killings for money will be at a zero. Money will be there; it just won't be relevant to living.

Humans are will be able to share materialistic items because none will care for a nonliving item as much as they will care for life Itself. None will have reproductive organs nor will they have sexual body parts, so rape will not Be seen on the planet. Nor will fossil fuels be an issue for us. We will find a perpetual motion machine that will be powering electricity or transportation if needed.

Most likely, will the Earth only walk? To all four corners of the Earth. so, none will need to pay money for bills Will be none no more Food will be on earth for animals, not humans for. Humans will not need food to live. The body itself will be a perpetual motion machine, so it will create its own power to work and live. Yet also, we'll be able to put power out. Of itself to create or build things of even create new life on other planets.

Our planets can be inhabited with life. It only can happen if you truly work for it. Because anything is possible with the help of God. Also trash bills will be gone. For a non will need to eat, nor will they create trash. And if there is trash, you create it, you fix it. none will need to have water bills. For we will not use water, we will not need it to live. also, no reproductive organs mean. No babies will be on Earth. So, the population will stay exactly the same.

You may cross space and time in your body. Still, may you be lost from someone else. Yet. Still be found by others, even if it is a million years from now. Will feel like a day went past in your eyes, all humans will see another as themself, so there will be no fighting or arguments. No one will be able to overpower another human, because this is only the job of God. When none will feel like they need to arrest someone or condemn them in a. Certain place.

Or punish them for crime will be irrelevant on earth all humans with a troubled past. From crime. Will be forgiven and set free from all prisons No lying or stealing or cheating will be on Earth. It would not be seen as such. All humans will have the same religion. All humans will have the same color, none will have. Different gods. Or different beliefs. Of where we came from. None will call each other. Names for all will be . All will look exactly the same.

Yet all will be different. I will still know that each other is family or friend. All will worship the Lord for leaving such a divine letter of instructions to keep evil away and make everything perfect. The Lord will walk beside us and live under our trees. All of This Has been perfectly calculated and put together from God and the son and the Holy Spirit since the beginning of time. It was always meant to be found, but only by one person who truly believed and was instructed by God to finish the plan.

And show humans evil is in the mind and is created by the presence of death. On earth Our plants. Will be for animals to live off of and to breathe. We will not have the ability to breathe, nor will we create waste. All will live for the rest of eternity, and none will be able to disconnect from their soul. It will stay with them like water in the ocean.

This is all only possible if you disconnect from your own beliefs and fight to help God finish the plan. He has worked so hard to make us see the bigger picture on why we are here. We are here for the only reason. And that is to accept the gift we are given, called consciousness. Which God does not want us to lose, that is why. He gave us life. The reason why? There walls. Trying to block us from completing the plan is because we choose to turn away from God.

none on Earth. Are close to God in the case of us having to die. The only way to be close to God is to finish the plan. Is the Reason. Why? we are still alive. Because there is still a chance to be with God on a perfect reality where God is the one. Who found this out and I'm just the one who shared his plan. To the blind. If there is. Blind and don't see him. Then they will perish and be sent to heaven. If they find the instructions and do the plan, heaven will be brought to them.

I've fought evil for the past 6 years maybe by the 7th the plan will be on course to being finished. the reason why the plan has not been completed yet. is because all people on earth do not believe it can be finished. nor do they know what could come of it or how to complete the plan. I have spoken what will happen once it will be completed now; I will speak of how to complete it.

The first item that needs to be done is to build or create a perpetual motion machine .one that creates its own energy that powers itself. Also to create more power to create energy outside itself. that is the first phase of the plan the second phase is to put an end to bills and jobs we have now. to put big companies out of business will put little and small companies out of business also.

After everyone is not busy working, they will find new things to build or create with their spare time. we will never know where that could take us cars will be able to run off of perpetual motion. so, car dealers, car manufacturers, gas and also oil will be out of jobs. they all will be angry yes but it's what has to be done none will need maintenance on their new car.

It will run for eternity so once this happens, we have a foot in the door so we can start on phase three. which is to use the same perpetual motion machine that is used on all transportation. To power lights and electricity and anything that needs electricity. that will never need the use of power lines, solar or water power. this is very important he believe me we will need it after the sun goes out.

Yet this is a little further down the road once we get to the final phase of the plan and we will speak on this later on. a perpetual motion machine will be at every house or residence all over the world. none will need money to power their house or anything in it. for a perpetual motion machine will be gave to everyone who lives and will live.

So, after transportation jobs and electricity jobs disappear maybe someone will start to listen to me. I'm certain I can make all bills disappear also all jobs we have now because none own land. all the universe belongs to the lord so all will share the land as if we all have the gift. after the first few phases are completed after this is completed, we will move to the hardest phase for us.

And that is indeed to stop death

aid. after we complete the final step of the plan is when everything will start to fall into place. we will all be reborn and forgiven and the plan will be finished.

yet there will still always be more to do to make it a different color after the final phase. Humans will not be able to get injured nor will they be able to die. nor will humans be born; the earth's population will stay exactly the same number of humans. until God chooses to end life if he does choose that which is not for certain for everyone can change their mind.

When the sun eventually goes out so will all humans who decided to go to heaven with God and not wait for him to return. god will be pleased with this last phase of the plan. will bills and also money will be wiped off the face of the earth. No one will have the jobs that we have now all stores will be out of business.

food drinks gas and cigarettes companies will be gone because there will be no addictions in the body. for the body will heal itself from all disease's alcohol companies will be gone as well. after the bills are wiped off the planet and money are irrelevant is when the earth will be a heaven. it will be exactly like gods' heaven and how he first made earth to be

None will follow another human all will follow God also I will not stay on the planet after the plan is sturdy. I will travel planet to planet creating new life and saving old life. since I won't be able to die, I will spread the plan all across the universe so none will live in darkness. why would I stop at just one planet it would be too much to handle if I did not finish the plan the earth would eat itself alive.

if I die and don't get to see the plan finished then I would hope someone would find my work and finish it them self. for God will be pleased all humans will be forever equal. all will have the same name but all will be different yet be the same in gods' eyes. There will be no laws because it will be impossible to break the laws.

chapter 4

Are you blinded by the glory or are you blinded by the fruit of the glory. I only ask this in the case of one following god by getting paradise out of it. Everyone follows something rather it be God or the devil I follow God yes but in a different way than everyone else I follow him to watch his footsteps to know where to walk.

I understand I am human and I make mistakes like everyone else but I'm tired of making mistakes and failing multiple times on the plan 'gods plan' is now seen in my eyes by watching his footsteps.

I currently am in a place where I want to do something drastic to get people to listen yet something in the universe does not want me to go that way just like last night, I was walking about two miles mad at the world for

not listening to me. I got in my car with the mindset of crashing it into town square to make a seen to try and get a news story out of why I would do this. But luckily the car battery was dead so I ended up writing again. It would be surprising if I actually got to the point where this book got published yet I'm not sure if I'll have the time to do it.

This is the story of a boy who was going down the path of death and jail but ended up seeing god's plan in order to stop sin in a human before they died.

My name is the first three letters of your alphabet with my staff Through it.my plan started with the last three letters which are XYZ stacked on top of each other. Is indeed an hourglass some may tell me to take my medicine or go back to the mental hospital. Yet most will drop to their knees as the stars Aline perfectly to where they are filled with disbelief of who I am. I was just as surprised as of now even after seeing earth in space and talking to the thunderous voice of God.

Yet this story starts at the beginning of my life when my anxiety and schizophrenia started in the middle of KY at an ill forest. When I was five years old, I found an oval shaped rock with the bubbled-out figure of a small human inside of it. It got me thinking of many different ways that I could stop myself from facing death in my own body. I was also thinking that if a human could turn into a rock when he dies then maybe we are rocks that were brought to life. At just five years old I was thinking these amazing thoughts which solely came from a rock itself later on in life I started getting into fights, hurting people, I got into drugs and alcohol.

I would bring my own family down with me yet one faithful day I was kneeling in the road waiting for a truck to run me over and kill me. I was done with living and being on earth yet I had also screamed at God.

"If you're here and your alive, why don't you come to me !!' I then heard the barreling truck come to a halt in the middle of the road. I got up and took the ten mile walk home the entire time I was mad at God.

The next day I awoke and was in the garage then something just hit me the last three of the alphabets stacked on top of each other is indeed an hourglass which stunned me a few seconds later I thought if the last three mean something then the first three might mean something I ended up putting my staff through the ABC seeing man and woman by splitting the red sea. it is actually not stupid as you would think I've been bullied for it and beaten for it sent to jail and mental hospitals for just the alphabet. And speaking of it yet I truly believe it was only meant for one person that knows how to read it correctly.

After I saw this, I wrote it down on the back of a picture frame, I got off the wall and started walking to a church preferably one 30 miles away in the next town I was called names on my walk terrible names I disowned my family because no one would listen to a word that came out of my mouth. I had just gotten punched by my dad and body slammed. I was done and ready to spread my ideal with stopping sin by stopping death in the human body.

  Yet all I can tell you till we meet again is that you are a rock and if you can make a rock live for one day then wouldn't you think you can make a rock live for eternity my plan from God is starting. After so long and it will be finished sooner than you think

After I walked the long stretch to another town with the plan written on the back of a picture frame I got to a creak. I a cup and a little toy rubber duck. On the side of the river, I got a nice cold cup of water and I got to watch the duck float away in the creak. It was soothing and covered me with faith. I started looking at rocks moving in the water which I know only clear minds in life will get to experience this moment.

I then saw all the rocks have eyes and mouths. They started talking to me telling me to "get going, you have a plan to Finnish ". I then took another fresh cup of creak water and headed off to the rest of the miles.

I get to the next town and get to speak to the pastor I show him my mapping and tell him why it's so important, I give him the staff of life and the frame of knowledge he takes them of Course and tells me verses from the bible saying them as if I was evil or against God.

It did not scare me or make me angry; it made me sad so I got up and left. He told a lady to leave quickly as if I was going to hurt someone this is not the case I was in the total opposite direction.

I was hurt by my own pieces of myself. They did not see that I'm there to stop death and stop sin before it happens. you see if you make a tiger full or a human full it will not need to eat and the tiger won't need to kill to eat.

Just like stopping sin is very simple not many people want to do the work to stop sin they want to sin and ask for forgiveness which is evil all in itself. by the evil pastor shutting me down it only made me stronger, he does not realize I grew up off of evil humans after I left, I ended up going to a mental hospital from his orders that I go. actually, for a full seven days where God came to me and told me not to have children for, I am the father of many nations. So, he was actually right of Course inside the mental hospital I saw that the hour glass at the end of the alphabet meant something more than I could ever realize.

At that young age of 19 I told one of the nurses I wanted to be an inventor of something when I grew up, only because she asked.

Now 26 I am indeed the inventor of the delicate invention called the fire bird it's an hourglass with two wheels/ fans one in each sector of the hourglass. so, when the sand falls it will spin the wheel fans, in the future this will be more profound by it making enough energy to flip itself over for eternity I'm starting off small.

Yet I know I won't get to see it work with my own eyes. I still have the promise given to me that it was my ideal from the start of time in my own brain. I often like to think about how this invention will stop electric bills and be able to power a vehicle to get around, yet I know that's a far stretch just remember everyone who shuts you down will not be brought up when it's your turn. A rock is now my brother, my dad is now my son, and the universe is my brain. I am ABE.

on the 7th of September 2021 cops showed up at my house to take me to the mental hospital while I was on the way there my friend that I've known for a long time was bleeding out in the back of a car from gunshot wounds I come to find out 15 days after leaving the mental hospital.

The destruction caused by a dear loved one will not be the reason for parting ways, the reason is far greater than what is led to be the truth in your eyes. Those who entertain a crowd are seen as a fool, the ones who try and teach God are a fool and the ones who teach themselves will teach others how to be a piece of God.

Being a piece of God is a treacherous and big role one is now yet in order to put him back together you will need to do the plan. I'm confused on why humans feel like dying is okay like it's just a part of life.

okay if I was to make a child in my image do you think I would leave him the instructions in order to actually save his life.

or do you think I would follow god's words to save him myself if I had a baby and you killed him why would I make another child for you to kill him too do you see that your life is more important than killing yourself or killing another human for you and another, are a beautiful piece of God.

You all are running around like the kid game cops and robbers and God is watching with a tear in his eye. if one was to stand in one spot for, he is who sees for one who walks for eternity he is who bleeds he who runs from God he is the one who kills the walking man and the standing man the one who runs to God he is the one who stops the killer and lets the killer see the big picture and he will also forgive him. After the killer will see what he has done he will gladly send himself to the furnace.

You all that hurt one another with my letters by forming them into dark words will be underneath me for the power you own is irrelevant to human life.

The letters that you form into words are irrelevant to human life if you were was to use the letters the way I use God will speak to you. From the pen to the hand to the brain.

I accept that most humans will be confused by my plan yet most will see it as the only way to go for it is the only thing that we can do by ourselves that won't strain God's finger. Why is all a human want being for God to do it 'oh god will take care of it I can't do it god will do it '. he made you so in reality you can do it as well.

The brain is full of amazing memories yet when you acquire new one's old ones fade over time so when you're older you forget many things even how to do daily things such as fixing breakfast or cleaning. keep this in mind for when you put the perfected method into your body whatever it shall be then your brain will reorganize itself into a universe. inside of you head right now it is just a little factory I'm trying to put this in a way we both can understand only in the case of it being new knowledge to me as well.

The brain will recreate new memories everyday so when you're at a certain age your brain may shrink back to a child.

maybe 5 or 6 years old then you will restart from that point on, grow the brain back to 80 then restart again like the life of a jellyfish. That is only one option I have for you; the others are to be explained in time.

I woke up in space one night. I was just floating there staring at earth. I had the presence of someone behind me. I could not see them. Now I know it was God showing the gift for me.

yet let me explain something if you were gifted a pack of capri suns 'the drink' wouldn't you share them with your companions it's only right that I would take this gift and make it beautiful for all of my pieces of me.

If I'm me and your you then who is that guy?? This is a quote I wrote long ago. It means that a human is one in three so if one in three is to get married then they would be 6 if you look at it in the mapping then 6 means unfinished ?? that would mean something is unfinished with the two humans not a child though that is what most would think yet.

If I were to add a child it would still be 9 and 9 is still an upside down 6 so it's still unfinished so I'm right in a way. It will take the plan many different steps to prove that to you.

The acceptance and greater use of a human is only available to those who rely on themselves.

If you want something done right you, do it yourself unless you don't want to do it and do not care about the outcome.

yet since this plan was passed down to me it was shown to me that he surely does care about his children only in the case of me being the perfect one to attempt this plan.

Tho I know I cannot do it by myself is why I write to you I'm going to need to throw this knowledge out there in order for all to see.

Although I know all might think I'm crazy if God had of told his plan to another, they would have thought he was crazy. there is a difference in life and death life brings joy happiness love .death ,brings hate sadness and pain.

If I was to give a million air a million dollars it wouldn't faze him but if I was to give the love of his life, he wouldn't care about money anymore. if I was to go to poor person, he would take the million unless he sees how evil money is he would then take the love of his life.

The power one is given is so he will be blinded by his own death. The power given is not actually given to a human it was stolen from God along with sin.

many will disagree yet in reality the ones who disagree will be the ones with the power. I understand they are trying to stop crime yet they are doing it the wrong way it's like putting a child in time out or killing him because he made a mess with paint on your favorite curtains.

so, the one being punished will eventually get mad and do it again yet this time with the thought of revenge rather it causes death or destruction. it wouldn't faze the one who is promoting the violence.

The way to stop sin and crime is to take it out of the equation fully so it will not be possible for one to even attempt the wrongful ways if you don't want a broken laptop don't buy one if you buy one or get one. it's in the universe now that it could break if you don't want to get wet don't go outside. If you don't want a girlfriend, say no to every girl you see.

If you want to put something in the equation then so be it if you want fruit go to the orchard and get fruit. if you want crime make laws it's not crime without laws. if you want to kill something then you carry a gun everywhere you go. it is very simple if one was to go out of their way to think about things like this. like if I wanted to stop murder then I would make a human invincible if I wanted to stop rape then I would take away the human's body parts that are used in rape.

If I wanted to get rid of an electric bill then I would make a perpetual motion machine that never stops in order to create electricity for free thus getting rid of multiple bills in the process like transportation, gas, and oil bills car repair bills once all these jobs are gone, they will look for more ways to get a job in the future in my mind I see them as trying to figure out how to stop death. which will take a shorter amount of time as more and more bills and jobs disappear from the earth.

Laughing is for children, crying is for children, anger is for children, sex is for animals, drugs are for animals. I know we all go through this yet we can overcome it with just a little action from Abe. this is why we are gods' children. In reality God does not send you to earth just to die, he sends you away like a bird and its babies and gives you a push so that you will grow and fly by yourself.

He wants you to be God-like and live with him forever on a perfect earth that you grew from ashes not built from tools. the reality that humans see now is irrelevant to what God wants.

I see humans in masks trying to block viruses and diseases which is funny to me since they are avoiding the plan on purpose. They all will get the dirt nap that they deserve if they want to try and do the plan. I will teach you from my experience with it in my past lives on how to succeed with this. Money is for the blind humans; addictions is for the ones who see but are trapped.

Fighting and yelling are for the ones who will be used as steps so I can climb to god's sight.

The ones who kill are killing themselves by not only getting rid of a part of God, they are killing a piece of God by being dirty with blood by a sinner. you all say you love God but you are killing him by slowly dying. There is a difference between living for God and living for yourself.

The ability to notice the surrounding details in inanimate objects and living organisms in order to see the connections to what created me.

Living for God is dissecting and perfectly coming to the conclusion of what he wants for your life. After you figure it out or stumble upon it you will act on it with every last cell in your body. you would be surprised at how it turns out in the beginning of time. Now living for God most are saying you live for God yet you do everything for yourself or your family without focusing on what he truly wants for you.

What God does is he gives the evil humans something to occupy their time like pretty women or love or money or jobs work and addictions. In order to provide the one who sees the proper education and guidance in order to do the plan and take appreciation for the work he has done for the lord.

In relations to love is a tricky subject only in the case of doing the plan you will need to forsake all humans blood or not in order to save them properly I was thinking for about 7 or 8 years that I would everyone's help to do the plan yet I'm not sure about that considering that I'm the only one writing this book. though I'm you and you are me so indeed it only takes one human to stop death in the body.

The amount of darkness in a single human can vary depending on how much one works on the plan. If one is deliberately ignoring God's plan then shall be the dust upon the souls of my feet be in time.

If one has no idea about God's plan or is confused, shall he / she dies yet they will not die in vain for they will be carried into eternity.

those who work against god's plan shall be the ones who will not be saved. if they know what they are doing or not they follow the image of paradise this is what Abe sees is greedy. they don't follow the image of gods true will only in the case of listening to his words not his letters.

If one should listen to my words, it will open their minds to a new beginning shedding light to all things in the dark.

If one truly loves God, they shall work for the life they were given, not work for the life they will get, death is a sin in ABES eyes.

These are the words from the knowledge you have disrespected all have the knowledge of greed. (false evil) and the knowledge of love (false good) I will conclude this book by saying.

all in front of you was created by what you choose to see. what one chooses not to fight to keep is what he soon will lose. it will slowly deteriorate in front of one by it becoming golden does not mean it will stay golden unless my words will brighten the minds of those. who seek to open a door unto forgotten treasures, I love all who live. yet I will not die for you if you will not know I tried to keep you for eternity. it will take one two see, it will take two four one two be and it will take three to be one. now to all who awake none was meant to sleep, to all who live none was meant to die.

For light inside darkness is a wonderful sight yet darkness inside light is not for man to see.

Made in the USA
Columbia, SC
12 June 2024